The Battle of Gettysburg
The Civil War's Biggest Battle

Wendy Vierow

The Rosen Publishing Group's
PowerKids Press™
New York

For Barbara, Andy, Max, and Alex

Published in 2004 by The Rosen Publishing Group, Inc.
29 East 21st Street, New York, NY 10010

First Edition

Editor: Frances E. Ruffin
Book Design: Michael de Guzman
Book Layout: Colin Dizengoff

Photo Credits: Cover (inset photo) pp. 6, 8, 13 © Hulton/Archive/Getty Images; cover (rifle) photo by Peter Latner, Minnesota Historical Society; cover (hats) Cindy Reiman; p. 5 Library of Congress, Map Division; pp. 7, 11 (top), 17 (left) Still Picture Branch, National Archives and Records Administration; p. 9 Print Collection, Miriam and Ira D. Wallach Division of Art, Prints and Photographs, The New York Public Library, Astor, Lenox and Tilden Foundations; pp. 11 (bottom), 17 (right), 18, 19 Library of Congress, Prints and Photographs Division; p. 15 © North Wind Picture Archives; p. 21 (top) © NARA/TimePix; p. 21 (bottom) © Herbert Orth/TimePix.

Vierow, Wendy.
The Battle of Gettysburg : the Civil War's biggest battle / by Wendy Vierow.— 1st ed.
    p. cm. — (Headlines from history)
Includes bibliographical references and index.
  ISBN 0-8239-6225-3 (lib. bdg.)
1. Gettysburg (Pa.), Battle of, 1863—Juvenile literature. 2. Gettysburg (Pa.), Battle of, 1863. [1. United States—History—Civil War, 1861–1865—Campaigns.] I. Title. II. Series.
  E475.53 .V56 2003

                                                                                    2001007248

Manufactured in the United States of America

CONTENTS

The United States Fights a Civil War

In the summer of 1863, the small Pennsylvania town of Gettysburg was the site of the largest battle in the **Civil War**. The Civil War began in April 1861, when Southern soldiers fired on U.S. troops at Fort Sumter in Charleston, South Carolina.

The main reason for the Civil War was a disagreement between Northerners and Southerners about **slavery**. The first slaves in America were people brought here from Africa. They were forced to work long hours without pay. Many Northerners thought that slavery was wrong. Many Southerners said that they needed slaves to run their plantations, or large farms.

After the battle at Fort Sumter, Southern leaders decided that their states should break away from the United States. They formed their own country, called the **Confederate States of America**. They elected Jefferson Davis as their president. The states that stayed with the United States were called the **Union**. Abraham Lincoln was the president of the United States.

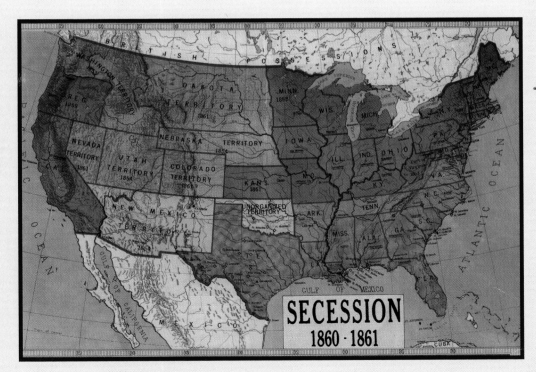

This 1860–1861 map shows the Union states colored purple, the Confederate states colored orange, and the border states colored brown.

General Lee Plans to Invade the North

Most Civil War battles were fought in the South. This was because the Union fought the Confederacy to take back Southern cities and land for the Union.

In June 1863, Confederate general Robert E. Lee decided to try new **tactics**. Lee was in charge of the Army of Northern Virginia, the main Confederate force. Instead of defending Southern land, Lee decided to **invade** the North. One reason for his plan was to give war-torn

This print shows Confederate general Robert E. Lee on his horse, Traveller, directing the Battle of Gettysburg.

6

Virginia farmers time to harvest their crops. Another reason was to gather food and supplies for his hungry army. Lee also hoped that Northerners would dislike having battles fought in their states and would end the war. He also wanted to draw Union troops away from the fighting in Vicksburg, Mississippi, on the Mississippi River. If the Union gained control of Vicksburg, they would control the Mississippi River. The Confederacy would not be able to ship or receive supplies.

This is a photograph of the Richmond and Petersburg Railroad Bridge in Richmond, Virginia, after it was attacked by Union soldiers.

Confederate Troops March North

In June 1863, General Lee's Army of Northern Virginia marched through the Shenandoah Valley in Virginia, toward Pennsylvania. The mountains near the valley helped to hide the

Confederates from Union troops. Union general Joseph Hooker's Army of the Potomac, the main Union army in the East, followed the Confederate army.

As his army moved north, General Lee found food and supplies in Pennsylvania. Lee would not let his

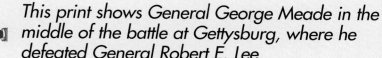

This print shows General George Meade in the middle of the battle at Gettysburg, where he defeated General Robert E. Lee.

8

Union general George Gordon Meade was given command of the Army of the Potomac three days before the Battle of Gettysburg.

soldiers steal private property. However, he did allow them to take U.S. property. This included items in U.S. post offices, railroads, warehouses, and other government buildings.

Many Northern politicians were upset that the Union army had not caught Lee. General Hooker was aware that Northerners were upset with his performance, and he asked to be relieved of his command. General George Gordon Meade replaced him. Meade took command of the Army of the Potomac only three days before the Battle of Gettysburg began.

The Battle of Gettysburg Begins

Neither Lee nor Meade planned to fight at Gettysburg. On June 30, 1863, Confederate troops, who were looking for supplies, approached the town of Gettysburg. At Gettysburg, they found Union cavalry troops, or soldiers on horseback. The Confederates told their leaders what they had seen.

On July 1, Confederate troops marched toward Gettysburg, ready to fight. The Union cavalry met them. Soon Union foot soldiers, called infantry, arrived to fight. Confederate troops outnumbered Union troops. They chased the Union soldiers through Gettysburg. Many Union soldiers ran toward nearby

This is a painted art map of the battlefield at Gettysburg.

The Gettysburg countryside, shown in this photograph, became filled with hospital tents for wounded soldiers.

hills to escape. By the end of the day, Confederates took over the town of Gettysburg and an area to the west called Seminary **Ridge**, named for a seminary, or religious school. Northern troops retreated to the south of town at **Cemetery** Ridge, named for a cemetery. They also occupied a nearby hill called Culp's Hill.

11

The Fighting Continues

On July 2, 1863, just after midnight, Union general Meade arrived at Gettysburg. There were now about 90,000 Union troops and 75,000 Confederate troops, all prepared to fight.

The next day, the Confederate troops tried to take Cemetery Ridge and Culp's Hill. Confederate and Union troops also fought for Little Round Top, a hill near the base of Cemetery Ridge. By the end of the day, Union troops had held their ground.

Many men on both sides were injured or were killed during the battle. Tillie Alleman was a woman who lived in Gettysburg during the war. She described the end of the second day of fighting by saying, "On this evening, the number of wounded . . . was indeed **appalling**. They [wounded soldiers] were laid in

The horror of the fighting that took place on the Gettysburg battlefield was described by many people who lived nearby.

different parts of the house. . . . I made myself useful in doing whatever I could to assist the **surgeons** and nurses."

The Battle Ends

On July 3, 1863, more than 160 Confederate cannons were pointed toward Cemetery Ridge. The cannons fired for two hours. It was the most firepower any American had ever seen. General Lee ordered General George E. Pickett to take 13,000 Confederate troops and charge Union soldiers at Cemetery Ridge. Pickett's troops marched in lines across the open field, a perfect **target** for Union troops. After the Union fired cannons at the marching Confederate soldiers, the Confederates changed their tactics. They regrouped and ran toward Cemetery Ridge screaming the **rebel** yell, a long, loud shout that some people say sounded like, "Woh who-ey." Most Confederates who reached the ridge were either killed or were

The Confederate troops under General George E. Pickett charged at Union troops, screaming the rebel yell.

were taken prisoner by the **Yankees**. Only about half of the Confederate soldiers were able to return to Lee, who took responsibility for the failure of the charge.

The Union Celebrates the Fourth of July

On July 4, 1863, Union soldiers cheered from the fields. The Union had won the Battle of Gettysburg.

Daniel Skelly, a boy living in Gettysburg on that day, was woken up at 4 A.M. by a noise. He ran to his window and saw Union soldiers. He saw "the Boys in Blue marching down the street, **fife** and drum **corps** playing, the glorious Stars and Stripes fluttering at the head of the lines."

Tillie Alleman exclaimed, "It was the fourth of July, and never has the cheering on that anniversary been more hearty and welcome than it was in 1863."

A unit of Union soldiers marched down a street in Gettysburg after winning the Battle of Gettysburg.

Independence Day was also a day of mourning. Union lieutenant Jesse Bowman Young described the day as a " . . . terrible national anniversary, with . . . horrors of the field . . . before the eye in every direction."

Thousands of men were killed at Gettysburg, and many were injured, such as this former soldier.

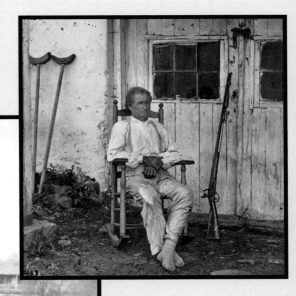

The Confederate Army Escapes

On July 4, 1863, General Lee stood on the battlefield with his wounded army. Of all the battles he had fought, Gettysburg was his worst failure. The Confederates gathered as many of their wounded soldiers as possible. They assembled a wagon train that stretched 17 miles (27 km) long, and began the trip back to Virginia. Because he could not get to them, Lee was forced to leave more than 6,000 wounded Confederate soldiers at Gettysburg. In all there were between 25,000 and 28,000 Confederate **casualties**. About 23,000 Union soldiers were

wounded or were killed. About 165,000 men had fought in the battle. More than 4,000 Confederates and 3,000 Union soldiers had died. President Lincoln urged General Meade to follow Lee and his army. Meade followed with caution. Lee crossed the Potomac River on July 13, 1863, and escaped back to Virginia by the next day.

Edwin Forbes was the artist who painted this scene of the Army of Northern Virginia, commanded by Robert E. Lee, escaping over the Potomac River.

Lee knew that he had failed at Gettysburg. He wrote to Confederate president Jefferson Davis offering his **resignation**, but Davis would not accept it.

 The Soldiers' National Cemetery at Gettysburg was established on February 11, 1895. There are 3,555 Union soldiers buried there.

The President Makes a Speech

On November 19, 1863, President Lincoln attended a ceremony at a cemetery at Gettysburg to honor those who had died in battle. About 6,000 people attended the ceremony.

The main speaker was Edward Everett, a famous speaker who spoke for two hours. Then Lincoln spoke for about two minutes.

In those two minutes, Lincoln gave the Gettysburg Address. It has become one of the most important speeches given in American history.

In his famous speech, Lincoln said, " . . . we here highly **resolve** that these dead shall not have died in vain—that this nation, under God, shall have a new birth of freedom—and

that government of the people,
by the people, for the people,
shall not perish from the earth."

Later Everett wrote to Lincoln,
"I should be glad if I could
flatter myself that I came as near to the
central idea of the occasion in two hours
as you did in two minutes."

👉 This a draft, or early form, of President
Lincoln's Gettysburg Address.

The War Continues

After the Battle of Gettysburg, many people thought that the war would end quickly, but it did not. The Union victory convinced many Northerners who had called for peace to support the war. In addition General Lee could no longer fight a large battle in the North. He had lost too many men.

While Meade and Lee fought at Gettysburg, Union general Ulysses S. Grant was fighting in Vicksburg, Mississippi, for control of the Mississippi River. The Union won that battle on July 4, 1863, the same day that Lee retreated from Gettysburg. Lee found Meade to be a tough opponent, but Grant proved to be even tougher. The next year, Lee faced Grant in several battles. On April 3, 1865, Lee **surrendered** to Grant. By the end of the month, the Union won the Civil War.

GLOSSARY

appalling (uh-PAHL-ing) Filling someone with horror or fear.

casualties (KA-zhul-teez) People who are injured or killed in a war.

cemetery (SEH-muh-tehr-ee) A place where the dead are buried.

Civil War (SIH-vul WOR) The war fought between the Northern and Southern states of America from 1861 to 1865.

Confederate States of America (kun-FEH-duh-ret STAYTS UV uh-MER-ih-kuh) A group of 11 southern states that declared themselves separate from the United States in 1861.

corps (KOR) A group of soldiers who are trained to perform a special military service.

fife (FYF) A small, flutelike instrument.

invade (in-VAYD) To enter a place in order to attack and conquer.

rebel (REH-bul) Having to do with a person who fought for the South during the Civil War.

resignation (reh-zig-NAY-shun) The act of quitting or surrendering.

resolve (rih-ZOLV) Decide.

ridge (RIJ) A long, narrow chain of hills or mountains.

slavery (SLAY-vuh-ree) The system of one person "owning" another.

surgeons (SUR-junz) Doctors who perform operations.

surrendered (suh-REN-durd) Gave power or control to another.

tactics (TAK-tiks) The plans to win a battle.

target (TAR-git) A mark or an object to shoot at.

Union (YOON-yun) The Northern states during the Civil War.

Yankees (YAN-keez) People who fought for the North during the Civil War.

INDEX

PRIMARY SOURCES

Cover. Engraving of soldiers fighting near a forest at Gettysburg, Pennsylvania. From the National Archives. **Page 5.** Civil War map entitled "Secession" by Albert Bushnell Hart (c. 1917). From the Library of Congress. **Page 7.** Photograph of ruins of Petersburg Railroad Bridge in Richmond, Virginia by Alexander Gardner. From the National Archives. **Page 8.** Print of Union Army General George Gordon Meade during the battle at Gettysburg. **Page 9.** Engraving of General George Gordon Meade. From the Ford Collections. **Page 11 (top).** Photograph of the Gettysburg countryside in July 1863 by Alexander Gardner. From the National Archives. **(bottom).** Art map of the battlefield at Gettysburg. From the Library of Congress; **Page 13.** Print showing soldiers in battle at Gettysburg. **Page 15.** A print from 1890 entitled "Pickett's Charge at the Bloody Angle." **Page 17 (bottom).** Photograph of Union soldiers marching down a street after the Battle of Gettysburg, moment's before Lincoln's Gettysburg Address; **(right).** Photograph of John L. Burns, the "old hero of Gettysburg," with gun and crutches. By Timothy H. O'Sullivan (1863); **Page 18.** Panoramic photograph of the Soldier's National Cemetery at Gettysburg, PA. (1913). **Page 19.** Painting by Edwin Forbes depicting escape of the Army of Virginia, commanded by General Lee (1865–1895). **Page 21 (left).** Photograph of handwritten draft of President Lincoln's Gettysburg Address. By Herbert Orth (1941). **(right).** Distant photograph of President Lincoln taken on November 19, 1863, from the Mathew Brady Collection of the National Archives.

WEB SITES

Due to the changing nature of Internet links, PowerKids Press has developed an online list of Web sites related to the subject of this book. This site is updated regularly. Please use this link to access the list:

www.powerkidslinks.com/hfh/battgett/